John Tschohl

MOVING UP

A step-by-step guide

to creating your success

1st Edition

John Tschohl

Minneapolis, Minnesota USA

Published by Best Sellers Publishing. Minneapolis, Minnesota.
No part of this publication can be reproduced in any manner or form without written permission from the publisher except in the case of brief quotations in articles and reviews. For information, address Best Sellers Publishing, 9201 East Bloomington Freeway, Minneapolis, Minnesota 55420, USA. Phone: (952) 888-7672/ Fax: (952) 884-8901, Email: bsp@bestsellerspublishing.com, Web: www.BestSellersPublishing.com.

Library of Congress Cataloging-in-Publication Data:
Tschohl, John.
Moving UP: A step-by-step guide to creating your success
p. cm.
Includes index.
ISBN-13: 978-0-9826369-2-3
ISBN ISBN-10: 098263692X
Printed in the United States of America.

"John Tschohl describes the cornerstones of success in four simple principles. If you are serious about moving up in your career, get John in your corner."

Harvey Mackay

Author of the #1 New York Times bestseller "Swim With The Sharks Without Being Eaten Alive"

"Moving Up provides a blueprint for realizing your full potential and achieving success in your career."

Marc Benioff

Chairman and CEO, salesforce.com

"Moving Up - the most thrilling way to live a life! John Tschohl is 'right on' with his messages. The human experience cannot expand until the consciousness expands. Have a purpose - pursue it with a passion - do not quit until you've caught the horizon!"

Dave Graebel

Chairman, Graebel Relocation Worldwide

"Moving Up provides the principles for success that work. Everyone can Move Up if centered on serving customers and leading without title beyond one's job description.

The only limitations we have are self-imposed. Moving Up by John Tschohl removes the self-imposed limitations people have and provides the roadmap on how to become indispensable and extraordinary."

Herman Gref
CEO and Chairman of the Board
Sberbank

"Moving Up is a book for those who are passionate about success, those who believe and understand, you never stop learning. It is a must-read book for employees who want to be A-class, indispensable, and valuable."

Eduard Kim, Founder and President
Technodom Company, Kazakhstan

"Everyone can be successful. Moving Up provides the roadmap on how to believe in yourself, remove self-imposed limitations and accomplish the dreams you have within you."

Maxim Nogotkov
President
Svyaznoy
Russian Federation

Table of Contents

Acknowledgement

I would like to thank my great staff at Service Quality Institute. Your loyalty and dedication is truly remarkable.

Pat, my incredible wife for 35 years, I am so thankful for you and for putting up with all my travel and my obsession with customer service.

I really owe my success to my Mom, Agnes Tschohl. My dad died when I was 7 years old and she raised me. I was the youngest of 7 children and we didn't have a lot of money but, I always felt we were well off. At a young age I mowed lawns, shoveled snow, delivered newspapers and did work around the house for money. My mom instilled in me a work ethic. She wrote up a contract and I could choose to do certain jobs and get paid. On a small sheet of paper (which I still have), she wrote that she would pay $.05 for cleaning the front porch, $.05 for vacuuming, $.05 for dusting and a whopping $.03 for cleaning the stairs. There were others listed but this was just an example of how she encouraged me.

Mom stayed at home to take care of me and my brother who was two years older. She always told me I would be successful and I believed her. Regardless of how she felt she would always say "I am fine." My mother died at age 102. By the way, my brother Tom and I took her to Alaska fishing at age 98 and 100. She caught more fish and bigger fish that either of us.

My mom nurtured my self-worth. She was always positive and never said anything negative. She got me to believe in myself. My grades in school were average but I had a mom who gave me more than money. I always wanted to be successful. One of my first goals was to have a net worth of $1 million by age 30 which I achieved.

Mom gave me love and a strong belief that I could Move Up.
"Thanks Mom".

Foreword

Great companies create great brands by creating *"Fans Not Customers"*.

"Fans" support your business, remain loyal and most importantly, recruit new *"Fans"*.

The role of an entrepreneur is to:

> Create a Value Added Model
> Install a Value Added Model
> Instill a Value Added Model
> Enforce a Value Added Model
> Improve a Value Added Model

And no one needs a *"me too"* anything.

Use John's ideas and experience to create the next great brand.

Vernon W. Hill, II
Founder/Chairman Metro Bank London
Author, Fans Not Customers

Introduction 1

"A man can be great if he wants to be. If you believe in yourself and have the courage, determination, the dedication, the competitive drive and if you are willing to sacrifice the little things in life and pay the price for the things that are worthwhile, it can be done."

Vince Lombardi
American football coach

My name is John Tschohl. I have spent my professional career helping organizations keep customers, build market share, and improve the performance of their workforce. I have been featured on major television shows from Good Morning America, CNBC and PBS to USA Today. I have spoken to various newspapers, radio stations, and magazines from almost every corner of the world. Senior executives want to know my 'secret' to building up a workforce of exceptional employees. After many years of conducting seminars and writing books for senior executives, on how to empower their workforce, I decided to write a book that focused on YOU. This book is for individuals who are tired of being in the middle; and want to move ahead in their career journey.

Perspective changes outcomes

Big dreams. Crazy goals. Insane ambition. These are my tools for success, the motivating factors that get me started on a path to what I want.

But these are thoughts that come to life when I put them to paper. I always write down a plan and then execute upon that plan. When the time comes to explore new opportunities, I write another plan and follow the steps accordingly. Most importantly, each time I write my plan I do so with assurance and self-confidence. I constantly look back to check my progress, because my present is a reflection of the lessons I have learned and the successes I have amassed.

Moving Up in any career takes belief, dedication, focus, and skill. I have been fortunate to encounter some brilliantly talented people in my lifetime. Sadly though, for every entrepreneur, banker, teacher, and manager I've met, few ever truly make 'big moves'. The entrepreneur still has only a half written business plan, and the chances of him opening his consulting firm are slim. The news writer who had plans of becoming Editor-in-Chief still sits trapped in her two-person cubicle 4 years later, not having worked up the nerve to ask for a meeting with her manager.

If you have a mind for success and you want to move up you need to start your career with clearly defined goals for accomplishments. Along the way, you may encounter obstacles, but without a plan on how to overcome them you will be lost. Speak with any CEO, President or successful entrepreneur of any company and they will tell you; they laid down a 'blueprint' of what they wanted to work towards. They understood that it was more than merely wanting to be successful; they knew they had to follow the moves of the people who had come before them, those who modeled success.

Moving Up

There is no shortage of great ideas, but there is a shortage of people who believe in themselves. It is time to swim in the sea of opportunity. Companies are scouring for 'rockstar' employees. They want members on their team who are not afraid to share innovative ideas, who are not afraid to lead and map out their road to success. Gone are the days of blending into the background of an organization. In order to move up, you must stand out. If you have a desire to become an entrepreneur, the same rules apply.

Your business cannot be like every other business it has to be distinctive, innovative, original, and command results. It is time to climb beyond the heights others have reached. Circumstances will always stand in the way, but there is still time for you to fulfill your professional dreams and move up! Listen to your dreams!

I wrote this book because I'm tired of watching life pass by the millions of talented employees and future business owners who – for whatever reason – don't connect their passion with their success. Life gets in the way, I know. Bills pile up, your kids need braces,

Your dreams for yourself and your family will feed your desire to succeed.

You owe it to yourself to fight the urge to give in and settle.

the furnace conks out on December 23rd, you get tired and you get used to your job and your station. Life happens to all of us and it can be overwhelming and depressing and make our dreams and aspirations seem so small. Don't you believe it for a second.

Your dreams for yourself and your family will feed your desire to succeed.

The dreams of the millions who came before you have built great monuments to success and innovation throughout history. You owe it to yourself to fight the urge to give in and settle. I know you have that fire in you for something. Maybe you want to own your own restaurant, or write a novel, become a missionary, or open the best dry cleaners in town, or manage a shift, or rise all the way up the corporate ladder and feel what it is like to sit in that comfy chair every day. You cannot do any of this without belief.

I want you to believe in yourself, take your goals seriously, and work toward making your dreams in both career and life a reality. I want to help you visualize your success, capitalize on opportunities that present themselves, and stand out as an enthusiastic and indispensible member of any team. When you do not live up to or function to your full potential you not only do a disservice to yourself, you let down your employer, your co-workers, and your industry.

You take up space for someone else that wants to move up to a position you have outgrown. It does not matter where you are in your career at this point. There are always opportunities to improve your skill set, and move up. If you are reading this book, you have taken the first step to drawing up your own blueprint, to making yourself indispensable, and to Moving Up.

Laying a Solid Foundation | 2

> *"In your life's blueprint you must have the basic principle the determination to achieve excellence in your various fields of endeavor. You're going to be deciding as the days, as the years unfold what you will do in life — what your life's work will be. Set out to do it well."*
>
> **Martin Luther King Jr.**
> *Civil Rights Activist*

I wrote this book with you in mind. I wrote each chapter, each sentence, as I thought about you, your personal goals, and your inner conflicts. It is my intention to guide you to the next level in your career.

Moving Up is about helping you actively seek out opportunities, recognize them when they arise, and then take advantage of them to best improve your position, your skills, or your future prospects. I know that sounds like lofty goals, but a solid foundation can make them a reality for you or anyone else ready and willing to improve their outlook and skill set.

Now that you're ready, where should you start? It's a question I'm asked a lot. At every event I attend or workshop I conduct around the world, the first thing anyone wants to know (and needs to know) is "Where do I start?" Look, if you are waiting for the next big opportunity to fall in your lap, if you're waiting until the stars are exactly lined up with the universe to start reaching towards your full potential, you will be stuck in the same miserable spot that you are in today. Let's face it if you want to move up the ladder of success you have to boost yourself up and start climbing.

There is no magical formula to moving up. It's a feeling or knowing that you want more, so you commit to doing more. Here's how I started my process. One morning, I woke up. My feet hit the floor; I walked to the bathroom, glared in the mirror and said, "Today, is the day I change my life". That was it; there was no magical routine. I made a decision to leap forward and I've never looked back.

Do not limit yourself.

All you need to start the process is to have a dream that you can turn into a solid, workable goal. Do not limit yourself. This step is not a time for pragmatism or practicality. Dare yourself to dream Big with a capital 'B'. In fact make that BIG with a capital 'B-I-G'. It can be anything. No endeavor is too massive, no distance is too far, and no height is too high. Where do you want success to take you? What does success mean to you? What would make you happy? I cannot overemphasize the importance of happiness in this equation. If you're not happy, if you're not engaged, if you're not consumed, then you're not successful. These passions must be part of your plan and must be a part of any foundation you construct. All of your goals and maneuvers going forward will extend out from these initial daydreams and mind maps. As you start to put all of this together think about how they fit into the four essential cornerstones you need to move up.

The 4 Cornerstones to Moving Up

"An extraordinary man is an ordinary man from out of town"

—Unknown

To be successful, you have to do what successful people do. Successful people are highly action-oriented. People, who are at the top of every profession, may not necessarily be the greatest at what they do, but these professionals share a not so common quality — they get things done! I'm tired of hearing people tell me what they plan to do, when they've made no attempts to accomplishing their goal. So many times, we plan to do things. We're going to develop a networking or referral plan. We are going to start a business. We are going to implement our strategic plan. We are going to have a meeting. We are going to make the change. Yet, when it comes time to evaluate progress there is nothing. But do we act on our decisions?

Nothing happens in this world until you make it happen. It is not enough anymore to merely have knowledge. Knowledge is really only power in reserve. It remains useless if it's not tapped into by applying action.

To be successful, you have to do what successful people do.

Successful people understand that nothing simply just happens. People must be willing to take calculated and consistent actions. The biggest risk a successful person can take is the choice to ignore their fear. Your passion is to improve your standard of doing things. You have to accept accountability of your actions and non-actions. The difference between success and a good intention lies in what we actually do.

The cornerstone of success is comprised of four simple principles.
- *Belief*

- *Dedication*

- *Focus*

- *Skill*

Every great accomplishment either in business or in life came as a result of someone making a decision and executed what they wanted. Nothing just happens, innovative, risk-taking people; make things happen.

Laying your personal foundation for success requires all of the above and even more. The process can be an exciting experience if you know what to look for and prioritize your needs. Constructing a solid foundation is a critical element of the process of moving up, and it must be done correctly to overcome obstacles and take advantage of future opportunities. Ask yourself these questions – and don't take them lightly. When you revisit your answers you'll probably find your blueprint right here.

What does Moving Up mean to you?

How do you feel about your job? Are you satisfied or dissatisfied? Why? What does "being extraordinary" or "indispensable" mean to you? What is your most extraordinary accomplishment? What barriers stop you from succeeding?

Successful People Believe

> *"Whatever you hold in your mind will tend to occur in your life…"*
>
> *—Unknown*

There is a saying, "Whatever you hold in your mind will tend to occur in your life. If you continue to believe as you have always believed, you will continue to act as you have always acted. If you continue to act as you have always acted, you will continue to get what you have always gotten. If you want different results in your life or your work, all you have to do is change your mind."

Billions of people fail to live the life they have always dreamed to live. They fail to realize their ambitions and give up on their passion as soon as they encounter the first obstacle. One of the leading causes for this attitude is that some people simply do not believe in themselves. Believing in yourself is all about being sure that you are going to do whatever you want even if others stand against you. Usually, when you decide to take a big challenge or to do something that people failed to do, you will find that everyone will not support your vision. When this opposition comes, don't take it personal. This is your goal, not your mother's, not your father's; not even your very best friend's. You waste energy, when you focus on what others think about you. What you believe, whether negative or positive will manifest itself. I challenge you today to take control of your thoughts – use positive thinking daily to reinforce the goals you have set and watch them begin to happen.

Successful People Are Dedicated

Successful people understand that dedication is non-negotiable. In my opinion, if you are not dedicated to what you are doing, you will lose sight of your goal.

A lot of the time, what we look to achieve is so far down the line that you can't see the light at the end of the tunnel, much less the end of the tunnel itself. For this reason you must be dedicated to your course from the beginning. A company exists through its employees and their interaction within the community. If the company's main purpose is customer satisfaction, then be dedicated to that. Let every decision you make be influenced by the goal of standing out and moving up. You must be dedicated to personal development, imagine how difficult it would be to grow in your field without continuing to develop yourself.

"Put all your eggs in one basket and watch the basket."

–Andrew Carnegie
Industrialist, Millionaire and Philanthropist

Successful People Are Focused

In order to give attention to something there must be a focal point. A focal point is simply a center of focus that someone aims for. The object in target shooting is to aim for the center. The same standard applies for success. All successful people have specific core centers called goals that they aim for. In order to find the center, they must remain focused.

When you choose to be focused, there is a sense of achievement and fulfillment. Unsuccessful people are often guilty of being unfocused. When our mind is focused we do not scatter our energy on unnecessary activities. Unfortunately, many people lose their ability to remain committed to their target. Whether it's with diets, New Year's resolutions, fitness programs or a renewed commitment to their jobs. They begin with great intentions, ride it for a while, and then start to slide. Once the newness wears off, focus starts to wear off as well.

Countless others lose focus due to stretching themselves too thin, with other commitments and time thieves. Too many things at once often leave people feeling overwhelmed and exhausted, which keeps them from producing the results they wanted. Determine what specific goal you want to achieve.

Winners think differently.

Then dedicate yourself to attaining the vision. Most people believe in having a back up plan. I am from the belief that those who rely on back up plans have a defeatist attitude. In the back of your mind you are subconsciously telling yourself it's okay to fail, because you have something to fall back on. Winners think differently. They fall forward, because they know there is nothing to catch them if they fall backwards.

If you concentrate on your goals you will succeed. Commit yourself to work on your goals and stay with them until it is 100% complete.

Successful People Are Skilled

Successful people have the right combination of skill sets in order to be great at their business. If you want to be successful, then you should strive to learn these skills as well so that you will be efficient and effective at work. Planning, communication, creativity, and productivity, all of these are essential to business and you must be well versed in all areas for you to be the best you can be. You must also have a passion for your work and a lot of motivation so that you do not lose sight of your goals. One thing that you really need if you want to be great is the ability to communicate effectively through writing.

Proposals, resumes, and reports -- all require good writing and a way with words. It is very important to be able to plan proper business strategies and projects. You can't simply start doing things without a proper goal in mind and the steps needed in order to reach such a goal. Without the ability to plan ahead, your business will burn itself to the ground. It is also important to plan for finances as well. Without good financial planning, you will be bankrupt before you know it.

In order to achieve a good productivity rate, you need to be able to manage your time, which means always finish your work on time and arrive at meetings on time and fully prepared. By always being prepared and on time, you will earn respect and a good reputation. Procrastination is the quickest way to kill your goals for the future.

Don't shy away from being creative. Creativity is needed if you want to work for a business that will draw customers in and be very successful. Thinking outside of the box is necessary, especially in today's economy. By brainstorming along with your trusted co-workers or employees, you can come up with great ideas.

Your Vision is The Blueprint | **3**

"People only see what they are prepared to see."

–Ralph Waldo Emerson
American essayist, lecturer and poet

Since you're reading this book, there is one thing I know about you instantly; you are ready for more satisfaction in your professional and personal life. You have made a conscious decision to change your path. You've created a spark, in your mind and spirit to be open and inviting to new opportunities.

Now is a chance to create a written blueprint for your life; which will guide your beliefs, determine your successes, and help you overcome your failures. In order to make yourself accountable to your goals, write them down, and place in a visible space to view daily. There are people who dream of doing something, becoming something, but in the end do nothing. Then there are those, who turn dreams into goals and actively pursue until they are accomplished. It is important that your goals are clear and measurable. You have to discipline yourself to reach certain benchmarks on your goal timeline. Hazy, unclear goals will result in the same outcomes

Create a written blueprint for your life.

as before– nothing. In essence, your dreams and aspirations provide the foundation, but the concrete goals you put together are the blueprints for your success.

I want to take you from the fleeting dream state to a solid and plausible future built on a set of actionable goals that drive your attitude, show you where to exert extra energy, and help you take those necessary risks. Your blueprint for success will be that roadmap. It will help translate your ambition into action and keep you grounded and focused. Too many times people get stuck in a place where they think they have reached their limits for growth. Once you foster a thought of defeat, and failure the outcome is pretty much settled. Putting pen to paper and identifying your hopes and objectives is the first in a long line of steps you can take to fight off those feelings of complacency.

Please try to understand the concept of a "successful life". When you think of success, it does not just mean doing well on the job, making more money, buying that vacation home, pulling that new sports car into the primo parking space, or putting your name in bold at the top of the letterhead. Sure, those things can help you achieve an amount of happiness, and they can be a part of your blueprint, and you can tick them off as you continue to triumph, but they don't define "success." The essence of true success is what you make of yourself and how that achievement reflects your vision and passion. Have you become what you want to be?

Success is the management of life that you develop, it is the character that you foster, and it is the type of person you become. This is the central meaning of successful living. Your success is not measured in terms of what you obtain but in terms of what you become, how you live, and what actions you do. Your passion should be as personal and unique as your fingerprint. No one can force passion on you. It's there, inside, just like your heartbeat. I discovered my passions when I asked myself what makes me feel most happy. You need to make an effort to discover your passions. If you love something, you derive pleasure from it. You are willing to give of your time, energy and resources without complaint.

A person that I deem to have been truly successful in their lifetime is Mother Teresa. At an early age, Mother Teresa found her passion. She knew she wanted to be a missionary to spread the love of Christ. She left her parents home and joined the Sisters of Loreto, a community of nuns with missions in India. After she took her initial vows as a nun, she began to devote herself to working among the poorest of the poor. Soon volunteers and financial supporters accompanied her and helped to fulfill her mission to help others. In 1950, she started "The Missionaries of Charity", whose primary role was to love and care for people no one else wanted to look after. She took her passion and dedication and developed a movement. She didn't become a millionaire. She didn't live lavishly, but she lived a life she was proud of and that gave her purpose.

Examine your current state. What are some of your quality assets? How can you use those facets of yourself to your advantage? What are some areas that need improvement? Think about the gaps in your knowledge or the deficiencies in other areas of your education or experience. Your personal blueprint will help you devise plans to fix those issues.

Success works from the inside out.

The road to success is a process. Once you identify your dreams, turn them into actionable goals, address the issues in your character, desire and skill set, and resolve to fix what you can, then you are truly ready to build to your success. Regardless of where you are today, or where you want to go, you need to realize that success works from the inside out. You have to be able to look at yourself and answer these questions. You must be able to get past any half-truths you've told yourself in the past and look yourself in the mirror with complete, unguarded honestly. If you're not willing to change then many of your attempts to better your position or work toward your passion will be ineffective.

Be Indispensable 4

"Being a part of success is more important than being personally indispensable."

–Pat Riley,
NBA Coach

Every institution or organization has indispensable employees who make a difference every day. Indispensable employees don't wait for instruction or direction, they figure out what needs to be done and they take action – because they understand and they are not afraid to discover what it takes to be indispensable. They can create order out of chaos, they can generate ideas, they can innovate on the fly, and they can connect the dots. They create value for their organization.

The brutal reality is that in our current economy, we are competing with other countries, that hire cheap labor. We can't afford to fill up cubicles with mediocre employees. Jobs that allow employees to do minimum work are on the verge of extinction due to outsourcing and cheap labor.

In order to be indispensable you have to do the work that your boss couldn't envision. It means you are

We can't afford to fill up cubicles with mediocre employees.

Almost all of the interesting jobs didn't exist a little while ago.

someone who creates a difference. These people have genuine job security, because what they do is scarce. They've chosen to leap unto the ladder of success and climb. They are eager to create and ensure exceptional work, unexpected insights and genuine connection. Do people come to you or do you go to them? Do you need a new resume? Do your references speak for themselves? Do you initiate or react? Do people seek you out and ask you to do something outside of your to do list? When was the last time someone asked you to come give a speech? This is the great part of your opportunity. Almost all of the interesting jobs didn't exist a little while ago. If you believe, no one is more qualified than you.

- *Figure out what you have a passion for (not the industry or the work) and then go do it.*

- *Decide to love what you do, because that's a big part of it too.*

Judi Sheppard Missett, founder and chief executive officer of Jazzercise, Inc., started teaching dance classes after retiring from professional dancing. Once she noticed a decline in turnout, she began to brainstorm and came up with an idea. The women weren't coming to class to learn the particular dance steps, they were coming to lose weight and tone their bodies. Sheppard Missett picked up the pace of her class, turned up the music, and created a fun class that was soon packed. She trained additional instructors to teach the routines she choreographed, which eventually lead to a franchise deal. The company now has over 7,500 locations worldwide, a clothing line, and an extremely loyal fan base– all from a dance class. She allowed her passion to lead her; to create a business that no one else could do.

After 13 years as an executive at Oracle Corporation, Marc Benioff left his position and hefty salary to found his company, Salesforce. com in 1999. He had a vision to revamp the way software programs were designed and distributed. He made replacing traditional enterprise software as his mission. 14 years later, Benioff is a forerunner of cloud computing and has been influential in driving businesses to transform by embracing social and mobile cloud technologies.

Understand that indispensable people never become complacent in their current role. They are actively reinventing, and learning more each day. Think about clothing designers. One minute people are willing to pay $400 dollars for their cutting-edge designer jeans, the next year those same jeans are on clearance in a bargain basement department store.

...indispensible people never become complacent in their current role.

If you currently work for a company that believes all employees are the same; you are setting yourself up for frustration and career suicide. I believe there are many companies who desire to seek out employees that stand out and make things happen. A young Vernon Hill was an eager college student attending the Wharton School of the University of Pennsylvania. He worked afternoons at a South Jersey bank owned by a local car retailer. His days of working at the bank allowed him to observe a retail principle model to banking. After graduation, Hill founded a real estate firm to find and develop sites for McDonald's. In 1973, 26 year-old Hill held a meeting with 15 potential investors in his next venture. He wanted to start a bank. 8 of the potential investors thought he was crazy and walked out. 7 investors stayed and the deal resulted in Commerce Bank opening its first branch in Marlton, New Jersey, in 1973. Commerce Bank grew from one branch in 1973 to 470 branches in 2008. He sold the bank for $8.5 billion and made over $400 million. His return on his initial investment was 470 times more! At age 65 Hill opened Metro Bank in London on July 29, 2010. Metro Bank was granted its license by the Financial Services Authority and was the first high-street bank to be granted such a license for over 150 years. Metro Bank is projected to have over 200 locations and $36 billion in assets within 10 years.

To be indispensible you have to think outside the box and commit to your dream.

To be indispensible you have to think outside the box and commit to your dream. Ideas are easy to come by, but execution of those dreams takes guts and a lot of determination. At the age of 18, Maxim Nogotkov, an entrepreneur at heart; began selling computer programs and cordless phones while in college. He eventually dropped out of college to devote more time to building his business. In 2000 he began trading wholesale cell phones. He would later found Svyaznoy a private phone retailer. Svyaznoy is the second-largest cell phone retailer in Russia. In 2010, Nogotkov founded Svyaznoy Bank in Russia. Svyaznoy currently has over 16,000 employees. Maxim was born February 15, 1977.

Believe In Yourself

5

"The future belongs to those who believe in the beauty of their dreams."

—Eleanor Roosevelt

First Lady of the United States 1933-1945

Are you happy with the many areas of your life? A little uncomfortable? Are you miserable? Feel like you have outgrown your current space? If you answered yes, to any of these questions, that's great news! It's great news because you have recognized that this current state is not the best plan for your life. You know this is not a permanent place. You are making a decision to move up. You have to be 100% committed to taking chances, to strike out on your own path, to unlock the creativity and passion that will thrive inside you. You have decided not to live in regret. Regret lives in the heart of those who saw the obstacle, but not the opportunity. Listen, problems never go away, as soon as you fix one set of issues; here come 10 more.

As the world changes, so do our potential careers. In the US many occupations are becoming obsolete. A significant portion of these outdated positions include clerical support and manufacturing

occupations, which are affected by the application of new technology that reduces the need for these types of employees, not to mention changes in business practices, and escalating plant and factory outsourcing.

People from all walks of life who are order fillers, textile weavers, telephone operators, and postal service workers just to name a few; are finding themselves questioning what to do next. You need to have a conversation with yourself and investigate the requirements for building on your success.

Success is about making a choice. It doesn't require you to quit your job, though it challenges you to revaluate how you work and question whether working for someone else, or your current boss is right for you. You need to face that choice with complete openness and honesty, and confront your passions with a cold hard look inside your own desires and ambitions.

My family and I were invited to dine with close friends at their home. Later that evening, their daughter asked for some advice about her next career move. She said she had a confession to make; she was wrong to start up at another teaching job this year. It wasn't the school, and was not the students, who were a great group of young men and women… it was her. Teaching was not her passion, and now she had thrown herself into an uncomfortable situation. She wanted to know how she could get out of feeling trapped in two worlds. She thought it would be best for her to stay and complete the year out and then focus on her. I instructed her to decide what she had a passion for. Write down some ideas about herself and try to understand what work would give her satisfaction. There is no reason to go to work miserable for a year, to try to prove how committed you are. The fact is your attitude will reflect in your work. If she stayed it would be a disservice to the school and most importantly the students.

You need to see and imagine yourself making that momentous decision or accomplishing your goals before you can take that next step and move up. You need to become an enthusiastic team player. Set up a series of well-defined objectives and standards that will take you down the path of achieving success. First you will set goals for yourself and then you will work on developing your skills by instilling a positive attitude about your abilities, using your time effectively and moving forward with cohesive determination.

Think about it. Every day, employers, customers, and investors make difficult business decisions about staff – sometimes as crucial as who to eliminate or reward. Someone at your organization or in your section or in your group is going to get promoted. They will get that raise that will make all the difference for them and their family. Someone is going to move up. It might as well be you. The real professionals, the truly indispensable employees get promoted before everyone else.

Someone is going to move up. It might as well be you.

Those of you who are ready to be the best professional and reach for the stars must understand that achieving your dreams will not occur without moments of hardship or conflict. Speak to any

architect and they will tell you, even with a blueprint, high-quality materials, and solid bedrock under their feet; some sort of challenge will arise. Problems and changes in the process are inevitable, and if you are committed to becoming more successful, you must equip yourself with the necessary skills to accomplish each task along the way.

Each of us possesses the brilliance, and the excellence necessary to shine. You can make valuable contributions and be creative. The art is in how we achieve the status of being valued. Only you can force yourself to excel and succeed, you must be excellent. I'm hoping you'll rise and choose to make a difference. Opportunities exist to change your life for the better. There is no better time than now to step forward.

I need you to sharpen your skills and increase your personal motivation. When an opportunity presents itself you need to be ready to act. You need to believe that you can overcome any obstacles that get in your way. You need to free yourself of your fear and limitations in order to enjoy what you do, to unlock the hidden genius inside you.

Jamie Stanley was a journalism major at a small liberal college in Wisconsin. She was a senior and would be graduating that spring. She was anxious about not knowing her future career plans after graduation. She had returned home to Chicago for winter break. After talking with a friend at a coffee shop, she picked up a novel from the bookstore. She found herself taking it everywhere she went.

Anytime she had a few minutes she would read. An older woman approached her one-day in the coffee shop and asked her about the book – she recognized it and was thinking about reading it herself. Jamie, went on to describe the book, the characters, how the writing style of the author was different, yet genius at the same time. She highly recommended reading the book. Jamie and the woman continued to speak. Jamie explained she was a college student, although she was studying journalism; she was thinking about other writing careers. The woman goes into her wallet and hands Jamie a card. Jamie instantly recognized the name. It was the author of the book she was reading. The woman went on to tell her that she also owned a publishing company for independent writers and would need an Editorial Assistant and wanted her to stop by her office before she went back to school. Jamie was stunned. Needless to say, when Jamie walked across the stage that May she had a new career simply by letting her passion lead her.

The key to Moving Up is thinking beyond your next paycheck or your next promotion. It's your future, and you want to move up. Imagine a frontline employee in a retail store selling clothes or shoes or electronics. They would obviously like to make more money and would look forward to any increase in pay, but where would they want to be in a year or in five years? How about in ten years? What can that employee do to make them Indispensable? What do employees toiling in retail positions, earning an hourly wage, dream about when they consider their future? What do they truly want?

The key to Moving Up is thinking beyond your next paycheck...

Aspire beyond your current situation. I want you to be comfortable thinking big and working diligently to achieve your goals and make your dreams come true. I want you to return to your written goals daily. I want you to constantly reassess where you are because it's the only way to know where you're going.

Be a passionate change maker.

Successful people, the original thinkers, the provocateurs, and the people who care, all have one specific quality that sets them apart: They can lead from the front; they strive to make human connections, and they are passionate change makers who will risk being shunned if they feel strongly about their position or their work.

The promotion starts in the mind.

I want you to understand your passion, and allow it to lead you to greater opportunities. However, if you need a reason to do your best, money can be a powerful motivator but should not be your sole source for attaining and containing success. There comes a time in life when you have to change the view of your position. If you're an entry-level executive, but have the passion to become VP of your department, the promotion starts in the mind. This doesn't mean you come to work the next day, walk into the VP's office and tell him you are going to be his replacement soon. However, you should start to see yourself in your dream position. If you are a teacher, but now have the desire to be an administrator for your school district; or perhaps you are a third shift call center representative, with a desire to move up into management the promotion starts in the mind. Your employer needs you to become more valuable.

The system you've grown up with is outdated. You were taught: show up for work, do what you're told, listen to your manager, fit in – and you'll be rewarded. It's no longer that simple. Those that succeed get ahead by doing more and working creatively. You no longer stand out by doing what someone else tells you to do. In order to survive and ultimately succeed in this new, technologically advanced, and innovative economy, you have a choice to make. Stand still by doing what you're told and just enough to get the job done – or be extraordinary by being faster, more remarkable, and more human. To get there, you first have to believe that it's possible and imagine your success when you take that chance, or go out on that limb, or stick your neck out.

I have a different perception of human nature. I believe that deep down in all of us there is an innate desire to continually learn, expand, improve, and succeed. Our brains strive for passion and creativity. We want to stand out. We want to be considered extraordinary. We want to be singled out as the most valuable players. We want more. The sooner you realize that part of yourself the sooner you'll do more than just follow directions. You will want a job where you are expected to be creative, where you are pushed to take intellectual risks, where your employer needs you to become more valuable. That value translates into promotions and better pay and increased satisfaction. That's what Moving Up is all about.

In order to believe you can be extraordinary you need to take a long, hard look at yourself. Where is the pride in your life and in your work? Do you take yourself seriously? Do you treat yourself with respect? Do you dress and groom yourself for the job you want not the job you have? Do you make decisions with your ultimate goals in mind? What can you point to with pride and say, "I did that"? How do you feel about yourself, your skills, and your career trajectory?

You hold the power to your success.

What I have learned in my 43 years of consulting, speaking and training is that successful people appear confident even when they feel less than certain. On their worst days, they still have an inner belief about their future and the position of their success. It is essential to the human spirit to feel validated. You cannot be afraid to stand out. In fact, now more than ever those who are motivated and committed to being successful will have to stand out and be heard. I know this sounds a bit cliché, but the sentiment is accurate. Whether you want to move up in your career or change careers or simply want to be the best you, you can be; it all starts with these the four words "I believe in me." You hold the power to your success.

Successful people won't allow low self-esteem or feelings of inadequacy flood their mind.

You have to conceive the notion of success in your heart before you write a vision for your life. Successful people have learned to focus on what they have and how these things will help to position themselves in a better situation later. They believe in living in the moment. Successful people won't allow low self-esteem or feelings of inadequacy flood their mind.

They encompass an unexplainable confidence.

In the early 1990's during the Dot Com explosion, hundreds of thousands of people were buying Internet stocks like crazy. One of the few people who didn't buy into the craze was Warren Buffet. At the time, everyone heavily criticized Buffet for his skepticism when dealing with these new stocks. A few years later, after the Dot Com bubble burst, many of it's believers lost a lot of money while Buffet ended up being the second richest man in the world.

In the early development stages of Microsoft, the company was going to be sold. The buyer turned the offer down because he thought that people wouldn't need to put computers in their homes. Now Bill Gates is one of the richest men in the world.

Self-Imposed Limitations... Expect More Of Yourself

6

"All limitations are self-imposed."

–Ernest Holmes
Writer, Teacher and Leader
Self-confidence is power.

Self-confidence is Power

This moment in your life, in your career, you have made a decision to dive into your passion. Expecting success from you is far more constructive than a continual fear of failure. Self-confidence is power.

As a child, I always thought the story about Benjamin Franklin was intriguing. From our American history books, we know Ben Franklin as an author, printer, political theorist, politician, inventor, civic activist, statesman, and diplomat. As a scientist, he was a leading figure in the American Enlightenment and the history of physics for his discoveries and theories regarding electricity. However, when you look at Franklin's upbringing, by all accounts he was 'a regular guy'. There are countless times in his life where he was denied access. Due to finances he was unable to finish his college education. Franklin educated himself and attained information that he believed was beneficial to know. When he was denied publication into a newspaper, he decided to start his own. He knew his abilities. He cancelled out negativity from others and he pursued his goals, becoming one of the most accomplished Americans of history.

Commitment is contagious and breeds effectiveness.

You determine your level of expectation. If you believe your life will always be on a road of mediocrity and failure, your subconscious will sabotage every attempt for you to accomplish a goal. Think about your job for a moment. If someone would ask you to list five positive attributes of your job, besides a steady paycheck, could you? If the answer is no, you'll be doing yourself a favor by finding a new job or career that offers satisfying, fulfilling work. I do not believe everyone enjoys every aspect of his or her job. However, I think the positives should outweigh the negatives or you will set yourself up for disappointment every time. The secret to true success is finding or creating a job that you can commit to doing well, and that offers opportunities for you to display your passion. When you do so, you bring out the best in yourself. Commitment is contagious and breeds effectiveness.

We often have certain tendencies that can prevent us from living up to our full potential. We are creatures of habit who get used to our environment and our circumstances. If we have a good stable job, we are more likely, to settle in than dream bigger and better. We don't want to rock the boat. We don't want to risk our position. We tell ourselves we're happy and satisfied when we feel anything but that. What holds us back is our personal resistance: the desire to curl up and avoid risk or failure. Its natural to want to feel safe, but we have to accept that safety will prevent us from achieving anything worth the effort. Only when we expose ourselves to the potential for failure can we see the ultimate goal, which is an extraordinary success.

When we are faced with new and exciting opportunities, we tend to find any excuse we can for avoiding them. We tell ourselves that we're not qualified. We tell ourselves that we're not good enough and would never get that promotion. We tell ourselves that our manager would laugh in our face if we asked for a raise. Resistance is everywhere. When you embrace it, you'll feel safe, but you'll also feel invisible and probably unfulfilled. If you want to be visible, you need to take a risk.

If you want to be visible, you have to take a risk.

These self-imposed limitations are the biggest barriers to your success. You set your own ceilings. If you think of yourself as a failure, you will fail no matter how hard you consciously try to succeed. If you do not respect yourself, you cannot respect others, and others cannot respect you. They will see that self-doubt. They will sense that fear, and they will be turned off by your lack of self-esteem. You can choose to be successful just as you can choose to fail by expecting failure. If you set clear goals, have self-confidence to act, believe you will succeed over

Self-imposed limitations are the biggest barriers to your success.

time; you will get to where you want to go. Sitting still is easy. Running can be hard work, especially when you meet resistance.

The limitations we impose on ourselves can be crippling. They can stop you dead in your tracks and keep you stuck in the same position with the same wage for years. If you want to move up if you want to make more money if you want to provide the best life for your family if you want to improve yourself, and fulfill your potential, you have to cast the limitations aside and think bigger. In my mid 20's I attended a 2-day seminar lead by the late John Boyle, founder of the Executive Power foundation. His seminars taught me how to use self-image and self-concept to achieve more. He believed you could unlock the power of your subconscious mind by reaffirming positive thoughts. His techniques proved to be significantly true in my life and career. Deep down you know you're good enough. Now you just need to show everyone else that you honestly believe it.

Whether I'm away on business, on vacation or speaking at an event, I take the time to introduce myself and speak to people. A small conversation can lead to a greater opportunity, just by saying a few words. Often when I meet people, I ask them what they do and where do they want to go. It's a simple; yet complex question with no definite answer. I ask the question to see how they speak about themselves, what they did for a living was secondary. Some, can instantly give a 30 second 'Impress-Me Hook'. But for others, my question is met with visible devastation.

Last summer while on a business trip, I met two men. The first was a new executive, Thomas, who introduced me to, Kevin, a new member of their organization's executive team. Kevin was well dressed, and after pleasantries, I turned to him and asked, "What exactly do you do, and where do you want to go?" Knowing that Kevin was in sales, I expected his pitch to be concise, sharp and effective. Instead, his response was fragmented, stale and unsure. Kevin did answer my question, but the tone in his voice and appearance spoke to me clearly. He wasn't confident in himself, or his ability and he didn't know where he wanted to go.

That same day I met another young man who was not a conference participant, in fact, he worked for the hotel catering services. On my way out, the young man stopped me and said he enjoyed my presentation on the importance of the customer service strategy. He reached out his hand and formerly introduced himself. His name was Charles. He explained how he was a junior at a nearby local university, studying business. He worked at the hotel; to supplement his income and even mentioned his plans to intern with a marketing firm that summer. Charles had passion. He exuded confidence from the way he shook my hand; to the way he explained his plans that summer. It didn't matter he was in a room full of business professionals with suits, and he wore a server's uniform with confidence. These two men, close in age, both with aspirations, but Charles stood out to me. He spoke about his future with certainty. He was confident enough to approach me, just to tell me what he thought of the presentation.

Impress-Me in 30 Tips

A great 30-second Impress-Me could open the door to your next career move. With a great introduction, you can market or sell anything. Your introduction has to be memorable and rest on a solid foundation to build relationships. Here is the method for creating an attention grabbing pitch.

- *Decide what you want to do and create some detail around it.*

- *Who is your audience? A potential employer. Effective introductions are created for specific audiences.*

- *Provide your audience with information, but don't bore them with knowledge.*

- *Why are you the right person for the job?*

- *When? You will never know when the time comes for you to use your introduction. Revise and rehearse often run it past a few people and get their feedback.*

Attitude leads to Action

Allow yourself success.

This process of positive thinking is not an easy task. Each day you have to make a conscious decision, to allow yourself success. Our society has this jaded connotation that somehow by wanting more, you are greedy. People blend in with the crowd, speak less and rarely voice their ideas. Expectation is not arrogance; it is merely a belief that you can attain more in your life. When negative thoughts come, you have to begin telling yourself that you are worthy. You have the right to want to excel in life both professionally and personally. Think about the dreams you have for your career, your life, and your family. Now start to see yourself attaining each and every goal.

Feeling good about yourself isn't something that happens just because you wish it into action. You have to work on making it happen every day just as you work on your professional skills. You have to take personal inventory on the way you see yourself. Look at the progress and possibly the lack of progress made in your professional and personal life and take notes. If you truly want to move up, you need to recognize that other people are not responsible about how you feel about yourself. You are responsible for those good or unpleasant feelings. How often do you give acknowledgement to yourself for a job well done? I strongly recommend that you take a moment and recognize your achievements. I have learned that self-praise always counterbalances the high winds of occasional failure or criticism.

The Prosperous Mindset

In the morning, set aside one hour for personal development. Meditate, visualize your day, read informative texts to set the tone of your day, listen to audio motivational programs or read significant literature. Take this time to transform your mind for the day ahead. Starting the day off well is a powerful indicator for how your day will run.

A burning desire transforms work into obsession.

Have you ever wanted something so badly that you were willing to risk everything to accomplish your dream? Sure you have. A burning desire transforms work into obsession. Your dream will keep you motivated if you continually remind yourself about what accomplishing it will mean, and how well you're doing at attaining it. You can't just put those dreams away and expect yourself to remember them.

You need to pull them down off the shelf every day, think about them, and remember why they are relevant to you. These constant reminders will keep you informed about your progress and motivated to continue to improve and reach that next goal.

Your thoughts determine your beliefs.

You have to be willing to claim your dream before you can plan for one. Your thoughts create your beliefs. Your beliefs determine your attitudes. Positive attitudes can determine whether you succeed or fail. Many people settle for the 'good enough'. "I've gone as far in my career as I can go. I don't see myself having a higher position in the company. It's too late to switch careers, or go after my real dreams."

Stop limiting yourself.

Stop limiting yourself. You need to be willing to step outside of your comfort zone. Visualize yourself in a new position, new career, and new business venture.

Personal Affirmations

One of the most valuable aspects of developing a prosperous mindset is the continual use of positive personal affirmations. Affirmations allow you to explore the infinite potential you have locked away inside yourself. Affirmations help you develop new beliefs that can eventually become second nature. They are positive sentences that describe a situation, which are repeated daily, in order to trigger the subconscious mind to act accordingly. When you are able to control your thoughts and emotions, you force negative thoughts to leave your mind. In time, you will begin to see yourself in a new light.

Success begins in the mind. Just ask Jim Carrey (actor) or Oprah Winfrey (Media mogul) they understood the amazing power of visualization and used it continuously in their careers. People who believe in their dreams look beyond their circumstances and give all their energy to their plans for the future. These types of people are set apart from the daydreamers. They will not detour from their goals no matter what. At the age of 22, I used affirmations to increase my success. Affirmations continue to play a key role in my life today.

Success begins in the mind.

I challenge you to repeat these affirmations with a clear and focused mind for 30 days. With practice, these beliefs will reign true in your heart and mind. It is important that the affirmations you repeat are aligned with your core values. Below are sample daily affirmations. I suggest you repeat at least one affirmation daily, throughout the day as needed. These affirmations are merely suggestions; feel free to add your own that better align with you, your goals and your passions.

Examples of Personal Affirmations

- *I love who I am, and I'm glad to be me.*

- *I am glad to be alive, and I've decided to be the best me I can be.*

- *Today is a good day. I'll have other good days, but today is special-and so am I.*

- *Today I've made a decision to win in my life.*

- *I can do it. Just watch me and I'll prove it!*

- *I am in control of my life.*

- *Nothing will stand between me and my goals.*

- *I am going after 'more' in my professional and personal life.*

- *I will do my best to be the best.*

- *I am indispensable.*

- *I can handle this.*

- *I am a great communicator.*

- *I am willing to give my all, there's a good chance it will work.*

- *I am good at...................*

- *I believe I am worthy.*

- *My unique and creative talents and abilities flow through me.*

- *There is a huge demand for my particular skills and abilities.*

- *I can pick and choose what I want to do.*

- *My work is enjoyable and fulfilling, and I am. appreciated.*

- *I earn good money doing what I enjoy.*

- *Wonderful new opportunities are opening up for me to use my unique creative skills an abilities.*

- *I am successful at whatever I choose to do.*

Setting Goals 7

"Goals are dreams with deadlines."

–Diana Scharf Hunt
American Author and Time-management guru

Setting goals allows you to increase your prospects for success by identifying opportunities that may arise and creating others on your own. An employee with a well-defined goal stands out within any organization. The technique is to set reachable goals. As you complete each measurable goal, your confidence increases and motivates you to complete more goals.

Setting goals means more than just zeroing in on a higher salary, but there is no reason that cannot be part of any plan. My father died when I was seven, and I grew up in a family with very little money. I was the youngest of 7 siblings. To say we were poor would be an understatement. In fact, what we refer to poor in today's standards, I would call luxury living. But, nonetheless, I had an incredible loving and supportive mother who cared for all of her children. As a child, I dreamed about becoming a millionaire. My mother always told me I could do better and would be successful.

My mother was my biggest supporter and fortunately she saw my potential from an early age and made it her goal to see me succeed. She did not allow me to compare myself to someone else, she instilled in me that I was uniquely different, and that difference would lead me in life. When I was 22 years old I purchased a self-development program on personal goal setting, self-image, affirmations and visualizations called Dynamics of Personal Leadership by Paul Meyer. The program was a pivotal point in my life. The principles outlined on the tape motivated me so much that I quit my first job after college and went into business for myself selling personal development and goal setting programs!

This is how it all started. I was a young recent college graduate. I was a sales representative for a large company. I had out-produced my supervisor ten to one in sales. I was daring enough to ask for a forty percent raise, but the organization procrastinated. During this time, I felt something at my core telling me that my potential would be stifled it I stayed with the company. Eventually, the company honored my request for a pay raise, but for twenty percent more. I made a decision to quit one week after I received the raise, and went in to business for myself. The first six months on my own I made $650.00, gross income before expenses. I was making only a fraction of the salary that I had previously. I was tapping into my savings and going broke fast. I started to have a heartfelt moment with myself. If I didn't start making delivering sales and earning revenue, I would have to go back to working for someone else. The thought of working for someone else both angered and scared me. I made a decision, that I would give my all and go all in to attain the results I needed to sustain my business.

I experienced hard times, but I didn't give up. When I felt discouraged I remember the voice of my mother telling me I was successful, I replayed my goal setting tapes over and over again. Over time, I taught myself how to use affirmations, visualizations and goal settings productively. I was hungry for success. I fed my craving by purchasing every tape and book on selling and closing. I learned more about selling and closing than 99% of other sales people.

Think about what you're worth to your company and compare that to what they think you are worth; and set a strategy in motion that will help you get there. Also consider what a higher rate of pay or a promotion would mean to the rest of your life. How would more money change things for you? What would you buy with a 10% increase in take home pay a month? Where would you go with more vacation days? Try to set tangible goals with real-world results and then review them daily or weekly. Your goals are your road map to success. If you keep them in front of you and refer to them often, they will stay at the front of your consciousness. Be careful when sharing goals with people. Not everyone will be supportive in your endeavors. I have found by sharing goals with people who are more successful than me, has helped me stay focused and on track. These people have always been supportive and are always open to give advice. Successful people encourage others to be successful. Initially goal setting should not exclusively be for career. You should also strive to establish goals in different areas of your life.

Let's identify 6 critical goal areas in a person's life:

Physical Health goals: Healthy living is essential to a fulfilling life. You only have one body-so make sure it is taken care of. This area will help you develop targets related to your diet, fitness and appearance. What would you like to weigh? What would you like your body to look like at your current age, at 50? For example, to keep active I play tennis 4 times a week. I want to reduce my carb intake, so I cut out foods that are full of carbs like bread. I have written very specific goals. It is not enough to merely say I want to lose weight, or be healthy. You must be direct.

Financial goals: Setting financial goals is not just a smart choice, it is the only choice if you plan on Moving Up. These goals are related to your material wealth and satisfaction in the present time and in the future. How much income will you earn this year? Will you pay off debt? Will you save and invest? What is your net worth today? My net worth when I was 22 years old was $2,170. Every year thereafter I focused on increasing my net worth not only for myself, but also for my family's well being. The only way to really measure financial freedom is your net worth. Do you own your own home? Is it the size you want? What kind of car do you want? Are you setting aside money for your children's college education? When my two children were about 3-5 years old, I started investing money for their college education.

My son was able to use $40,000 of his college fund to make a down payment on his house, during his sophomore year in college. My daughter still has about $38,000 in her college fund saved. Moving Up allows greater financial freedom and your ability to take better care of your family. You need to have definite goals for increasing your income. If you have no pressing dreams for more income your goals will not be reached. I cannot stress enough the importance of setting clearly defined goals. Write down what financial goals you want to see accomplished. Most people spend their income few rarely invest. The only way to increase your wealth is through investments. I invest 80% of my income. For some of you, this may be a bit extreme, start small. Speak with a financial planner and begin investing in yourself and family for the future.

Family goals: You want the best for your family, now it is time to take action and define goals for your family. These goals will build trust and a strong unit between all of you. Establish goals that will strengthen and enhance your relationship with your spouse, children, siblings and parents. It is important that your spouse is in agreement with your goals. Your spouse is your helpmate and biggest supporter. When there is a breakdown in communication, there will be no growth in the accomplishments of your goals. If your family dynamic is in turmoil, it will negatively impact other areas of your life and distract you from accomplishing your other goals. Make it a point to spend time with your family.

Spiritual goals: When you feed your soul, you feed your goals. Each person will have goals that are specific to them and their needs. These goals build peace of mind, heart and spirit. When we have peace within, amazing results appear in every area of our lives. Ethics and integrity is extremely critical to your success. Jack Welch, former CEO of General Electric, said the most difficult challenge he had was having a high performance worker who was weak in ethical behavior. That type of unethical behavior had no place in his company; they had to go. Ask yourself these questions: What can I do each day to gain spiritual growth? What spiritual resources will I study/meditate to gain a deeper understanding of my faith?

Remember your goals need to be crystal clear and measurable. Vague goals produce vague results. Think about everything that your goals can affect. Play out the scenarios. Your family, financial well-being, personal health and fitness, spiritual and educational development are all connected. More money won't help you if you're in poor health. Family stress can impact your job and income.

If you're not happy with your current position, you need to be the one to make the change. If one set of goals isn't working out, reorient yourself. You should be constantly reevaluating your goals and finding new ways to make them your reality. Remember, you can't get there if you don't believe it first. Your dreams will wither and die on the vine without some self-esteem and visualization to fertilize their growth.

Mental/ Educational Goals: In order to Move Up you need to improve your leadership and management skills. Investing in yourself is the safest investment you can make. I strongly suggest attending workshops that will enhance your skills i.e. take a certification course in your specific area. This certification could very well lead to a promotion and higher pay. My mental/education goals include, reading 12 personal development books a year on leadership, management, customer service, sales and personal development. It is imperative that you set goals to read books, magazines, blogs and articles on areas you want to improve.

Social goals: In my 40 some years of business experience. I have come to realize that success will be measured by your personal achievements, as well as, your contribution to society.

As you begin to review your goals, you will notice your goals are actually interdependent. For example, how well you will do financially depends on your advancement in your career. Likewise your career, relationships will alter the progression of your personal and spiritual development as well as your physical well-being. I have always been involved in major leadership roles. As a teenager, these types of roles allowed me to help others and gain self-confidence and a positive self-image. I continued to acquire leadership positions on my college campus at the University of St. Thomas. I created a College Republicans club. My senior year, I became Chairman of the Minnesota College Republicans. During my senior year of college, I spent tireless hours working for a group I started called the Coalition for Lowering the Voting Age. We had over 50,000 college students support it. As an adult, I volunteered to serve as finance chairman for my Congressman Bill Frenzel for 16 years. Each organization that I either created or joined I did so because I had a passion to add to the cause.

This passion, dedication and hard work carried on into my personal and professional life. When you are setting goals for your life, be sure to think about other ways you can be of service to others. I believe this is when you will be able to enjoy a fulfilling and balanced successful life.

Writing goals

Read over the six rules to see if your goal passes the rules test.

Rules to Writing Goals

1. **Make sure the goal is something you truly want** - List goals that resonate with you. You want to achieve the goal because you desire to fulfill your dream.

2. **Write the goal in a positive tone** - Write the goal as if it has already happened. "I look forward to the day when I receive my Master of Business Administration degree." Rather than " It would be nice to have a Master of Business Administration Degree."

3. Be specific about your goal - Goals should not be generalities. A goal like "Find a better job and make more money" is not specific enough.

4. Place a time frame on your goal - a deadline will keep you focused. Goals without a time frame will result in ambitious dreaming without any accomplishment.

5. Make the goal measurable - Each of your goals needs to be assigned both a measurable unit (to quantify success) and a unit of time (days, weeks, months, hours etc., which you'll measure your success). For example I want to lose 15 pounds in 3 months before my birthday" shows the specific target to be measure. "I want to lose weight" is not as measurable.

6. The goal must be realistic - The goal needs to be realistic for you and where you are currently. A goal of never watching television again may not be realistic for you if you really enjoy watching your favorite television programs. For instance, it may be more realistic to set a goal of reading one hour a day before you watch television. You can then choose to work towards reducing the amount of television consumption gradually when this feels realistic for you.

- *Use the following sheet to write down your goals. You will probably have tons of goals for each category. You can make copies of the following goal sheets, or write your own on a separate sheet of paper.*

- *I strongly suggest in the beginning stages of writing your goals; you limit yourself to 5 goals in each category. Once a goal has been accomplished from your list within a specific category add another. This will keep your list manageable and encouraging as you begin to check off your list of complete goals.*

- *Each year on January 1st since 1970, I write my business/game plan for the year in every area of my life.*

Goal Setting: Worksheet

State your goal:

_____

_____

_____

What action(s) are required to accomplish this goal?

_____

_____

_____

How will you know when you reach your goal? What will success look like?

_____

_____

_____

Why is your goal important to you?

_____

_____

_____

What is your timeline for reaching your goal?

_____

_____

_____

List 3 steps you need to take to reach your goal:

_____

_____

_____

List potential barriers and any strategies for overcoming them:

_____

_____

_____

Don't be afraid of failure.

When setting your goals and visualizing your success, don't be afraid of failure. In fact, fear of failure drives many successful people. Think about successful people – in all industries and walks of life. One thing they share in common: they think about failure differently. Successful people consider failure to be a learning opportunity, a chance to assess a different path to success. In every failure – or success – resides a life lesson.

That's a different approach, one that de-emphasizes defeat and focuses on the end we all seek – success. So when we look at failure as a learning opportunity, we can see tactics that didn't work and opportunities that might succeed next time.

Overcoming Your Fear – Conquering Your Setbacks

8

"The only thing we have to fear is fear itself."

—**President Franklin D. Roosevelt.**
32nd President of the United States of America

Fear is one of the most powerful and dangerous emotions in the business world. You can easily overcome a lack of skill, or a gap in your knowledge with hard work and perseverance. But fear can be pervasive and difficult to conquer. Resistance hides fear. The more you move to overcome resistance, the more you expose yourself to a fear of failure – and to succeed you'll need to fight even harder.

Fear is often why we do not readily embrace our dreams. It keeps us from seeing ourselves get

Fear is often why we do not readily embrace our dreams.

promoted. Our fears tell us we aren't good enough, or that we will fail if we reach too far. Fear is the real enemy – it's natural to feel anxious about our work and our performance, but we have to realize that it's a wasted feeling and that it only holds us back. Fear paralyses us and keeps us from achieving success. The reason it keeps you awake at night is that fear prevents you from moving forward. So what we have to do is first recognize fear for what it is - an exaggeration of the worst possible scenario. When we embrace fear, we look for safety and then we stall out.

When we resist or overcome fear; we move forward with our goals in sight and achievement in mind. Fear takes away your power; overcoming fear empowers you. It's impossible to Move Up if you can't resist your fear.

Don't fear your mistakes.

Don't fear your mistakes. Fear only the absence of creative, constructive, and corrective responses to mistakes. Expecting success is far more constructive than giving in to a fear produced by an acute awareness of personal inadequacies, doubts, and fear of failure.

Overcoming your fear and self-imposed limitations can set you apart from your co-workers on the job. It is also essential if you want tackle the next goal on your list and dream bigger.

Fear Reflection Questions

1. What barriers prevent you from succeeding or achieving more on the job?

_____

_____

_____

2. How can your organization help you overcome those barriers?

_____

_____

_____

3. What self-imposed limitation affects you the most? Why?

_____

_____

_____

4. What do you need to help you conquer those fears in order to succeed?

_____

_____

_____

The Process Of Self- Assessment

9

"Too many people overvalue what they are not and undervalue what they are."

–Malcolm S. Forbes

American business leader, owner-publisher of Forbes magazine

I cannot stress this enough. We are all a work in progress. But if you don't take the time to critique yourself and your behaviors along the way, you run the risk of becoming complacent.

Improve your relationships with people because it is your relationship with people that make you successful in both life and business. If you discover that the same issues continue to arise, it's time for some tough self-examination. The most needed and essential workers are so hard to replace, so dangerous to lose, and so vital to an organization's success that they might as well be irreplaceable. Very few of us set out to be average or to be normal. We want to be indispensable, creative, and irreplaceable, but we don't know where to start.

You start by taking a look at yourself and your skill set. You can't just take a good, long look in the mirror. You honestly need to assess yourself as objectively as you can. This is about more than looking deep inside your soul and dragging your self-confidence to the forefront, this is about dissecting your talents, identifying your deficiencies, and making a plan for further development. You can do this with an honest and accurate self-assessment.

Do you think about your dreams?

Think about your job and your life and thoroughly examine where you stand. Are you truly happy, or are you just content with your station in life? Are you inspired on a daily basis, or are you just safe in your position and comfortable being anonymous? Do you want to make more money or earn a promotion, or are you simply satisfied just scraping by on what you have because you don't want to rock the boat? Do you think about your dreams very often, or have you buried all of them beneath your indecisiveness and the crushed aspirations of your past?

You must believe it is possible, and you are capable.

A self-assessment will help you remember those dreams and bring them to the forefront of your goals. It can get you believing in yourself and your talents again. In order for you to accomplish anything and make a huge life change, you must first believe it is possible, and you are capable. Examining yourself and assessing your skills is the first step.

An accurate and honest self-assessment can be difficult. As human beings, we tend to immediately come to our own defense when criticized, even when we are the ones criticizing ourselves. We make excuses for our actions or inadequacies. We explain our faults and mistakes. We shift blame away from ourselves to make us look good in our own eyes. We all do it, but you need to avoid these traps if you are going to produce an honest and actionable self-assessment.

Unless you are able to honestly observe and scrutinize your attitude, your work ethic, your strengths, your aspirations, and your opportunities for improvement, you will never be able to live up to your potential. Your dreams will never truly come true. They will crash and burn within the wreckage of your damaged psyche. If you cannot be honest with yourself, who can you be honest with? This goes for your positive qualities, as well. We often tend to diminish our own accomplishments and talents to others and to ourselves. Use your self-assessment to highlight those strengths and successes so you can create accurate and manageable goals going forward.

A good self-assessment will allow you to measure your progress and compare yourself with yourself, rather than against the success of other friends, family members or co-workers. It will hold your performance and advancement up to your own desires. It will help you become more proactive with your career and personal trajectory and set you apart as a valuable commodity that any organization would be more than happy to employ and promote.

Use this form to create a self- assessment that you can use to further develop your strengths and improve your areas of weakness. In every category, circle the number for the statement that best describes your behavior or attitude.

Self-Assessment Worksheet

SECTION I	
Attitude: • Aloof, uneasy, pessimistic • Helpful, but not proficient • Positive, helpful, confident, and fast	Comments
Awareness of customer needs: • Shows little concern • Takes steps to try to improve • Consistently improving performance	Comments
Sincerity of Motives: • Pays little attention during projects/tasks • Shows some concern and sincerity • Displays commitment to quality	Comments
Accountability: • Blames others for personal deficiencies • Usually takes responsibility for performance • Consistently accountable for the quality and delivery of all projects and tasks	Comments
Empowerment: • Rarely makes decisions • Makes some choices • Consistently makes informed decisions that benefit a project or task	Comments

Subtotal

SECTION II **Awareness of Individual Job Importance:** • Shows little concern • Somewhat unsure of significance • Shows pride and acts professionally	Comments
Overcome Barriers: • Does not work to succeed despite barriers • Has some success overcoming barriers • Consistently able to avoid barriers and overcome those that do get in the way	Comments
Organizational Skills: • Unorganized • Somewhat organized, but often inefficient • Exhibits helpful organizational skills built on logic and understanding	Comments
Ability to Identify Opportunities for Improvement: • Never Improves • Occasionally sees opportunities and takes action • Consistently recognized for improvements	Comments
Staying informed: • Does not know new company information • Knows some new company information • Stays very informed and up-to-date	Comments
Displays Trust in Company/Management: • Shows a complete lack of trust • Shows some trust; not there yet • Displays complete trust	Comments
Delegates Authority: • Never delegated authority • Sometimes delegates authority • Always delegates authority when needed	Comments

Subtotal

SECTION III **Quality of Performance:** • At or below minimum requirements • Generally good performance; strives for improvement • Fast, efficient, and reliable	Comments
Ability to Handle Problem Situations: • Experiences frustration; makes no attempt to handle problems • Attempts to handle situations • Usually succeeds in solving problems	Comments
Over Delivers on expectations: • Rarely meets expectations • Consistently meets expectations • Routinely over delivers and exceeds expectations	Comments
Ability to Handle Stress: • Unable to perform under pressure • Requires reassurance and feedback • Independently able to recover and regain positive attitude	Comments
Ability to Satisfy the Demands of the Job: • Uncertain and hesitant in discovering needs • Demonstrates good questioning and listening skills • Takes responsibility, works efficiently, and displays an expert understanding	Comments

Subtotal

Overall Assessment	*Number of Points*
Section I:	_____
Section II:	_____
Section III:	_____
TOTAL	_____

Self-Assessment Standards

Score	Rating	Evaluation
17-22	Below Standard	You need to decide if you're on the right career path. You need more professional development training.
23-28	Occasionally Below Standard	Address the areas you need to improve. Write a plan of action to measure your improvement. You need more professional development training.
29-37	Standard	You satisfactorily perform all aspects of your job and consistently meet performance standards. You are on your way to a management level. Needs advance professional development training.
38-45	Excellent	You are an excellent team leader and have the passion and knowledge to Move Up to executive level. Needs advance professional development training.
46-51	Outstanding	Demonstrates executive level attitude, skills, and judgment. Needs advance professional development training.

Assessment Date: _____

Self-Assessment Reflection

Below are questions to help you identify areas for self-improvement. Ask yourself these questions and be truthful as possible.

- *How do you feel about your overall self-assessment score?*

- *What area on the self-assessment do you consider to be your greatest strength? Why?*

- *What area on the self-assessment do you consider to be your greatest weakness? Why?*

- *Take a few minutes to put together an action plan based on your self-assessment that will help you improve your score when you next assess yourself in six months. Where can you see the biggest improvement in your score? How can you increase your scores in those sections and areas?*

- *How do you think you can translate your self-assessment score into success or improvement on the job?*

Seeking Constructive Feedback | **10**

"A person who is his own counselor frequently has a fool for a client".

–Unknown

Constructive feedback enables you to understand what you are doing and how you are doing it. When you open yourself up to an objective and honest self-assessment, it can be difficult to find a baseline or jumping off point for your analysis.

Seek out constructive feedback from your managers, co-workers, friends, family members, and maybe even a few customers or clients that you trust. The key is to build up a network of people who are far more successful than you. Listen to their advice, take notes and implement their suggestions. Do not listen to people who are all talk and no action. I cannot tell you how many people try to give me financial advice that have not followed their own. I'm sure they mean well, out of courtesy I listen, but I have no intention of taking their advice. You can't get to the next level in your life, with people who are on the

Build up a network of people who are far more successful than you.

same level as you. Many employees dread receiving feedback or criticism. They think of these moments as opportunities to hear what they're doing wrong. It can increase your anxiety and put you on the edge. No one likes to be criticized, but you must embrace the opinions and expertise of others in your field or who know you in order to move up, increase your earning potential, and begin to make a life change. Constructive feedback is the best way for you to begin the process of assessing your talents, performance, and skill level, and in furthering your development.

I cannot emphasize enough the importance of taking notes when receiving feedback so you can refer to them later and try to align them with the deficient areas you identify in your self-assessment. Try to figure out if others have a similar picture of you as you have of yourself. This will show you that your self-assessment is accurate and that those around you have similar perceptions. If their idea of you is radically different from the information you're working from on your self-assessment then you will have even more work to do. You will need to find where their perceptions and your own diverge and how to fill in those gaps moving forward. Again, rely on your self-assessment information.

In addition to your friends and colleagues, your organization may have a formal structure for providing feedback, such as an annual performance review. Make sure you get a copy whenever a review is conducted so you can compare it to your own and track your progress and development. Go over it, ask questions, and refer to previous reviews to help construct more accurate goals. Consider what your managers and co-workers believe to be your strengths and weaknesses and think about how that balances with your own self-image.

Immediately after receiving any feedback you need to start to create a plan of attack to improve on some of the shortcomings that are brought to light, and build on the abilities where you show promise. Accumulate all of the feedback and apply it to your self-assessment and construct a reference for future achievement. Approach any feedback, whether conducted by a manager, a co-worker, or yourself, with honesty and openness. You need to understand your own talents and expertise, as well as any deficiencies so you can build yourself up and turn yourself into an indispensable employee. It is essential you listen to all the information that is given to you. We all enjoy hearing someone tell us what our strengths are, but it is equally beneficial to listen to others explain some of our weaker areas. If your goal is to grow as a professional and as a person, you have to be willing to listen and change. Receiving feedback is a positive progression towards success, so treat it as such. Perhaps, your current employer does not have a review process. Request a performance review anyway. Ask them what you can do to improve your performance in order to Move Up.

In my career, I have made a strict decision to only listen to those much more successful than me in that particular area I want to improve. For example, I enjoy fishing, however, I have friends that are light years ahead of me. So, I listen to their advice and the technique I should use. When hunting I have a friend that I continually listen to so I can improve my shooting skills. When skiing I ask friends that are terrific skiers to give me pointers. For financial advice, I have only listened to two people who were dramatically more successful than me. I sought individuals who were 20 years older than me. They appreciated my willingness to seek them out, listen to their advice and followed up with them on my progress.

The late Paul Meyer's the founder of Success Motivation Institute who owned over 39 companies and created incredible wealth was only asked by two people for advice. I was one of them. My good friend Don Charleston who recently died at age 85 always gave me advice on investments in high paying dividend utility stocks. He had investments exceeding $1 million dollars and managed his accounts daily. When I had an extra $10,000 or more, he would tell me what to invest into. I would show him my investments every year, and he would give me even more help. I make it a point never to listen to those who are not in a position of extreme success.

REFLECTIONS
Points to Remember

- *A self-assessment is about dissecting your talents, identifying your deficiencies, and making a plan for further development*

- *A self-assessment will help you remember your dreams and bring them to the forefront of your goals*

- *Unless you can honestly observe and scrutinize your attitude, your work ethic, your strengths, your aspirations, and your opportunities for improvement, you will never be able to live up to your potential*

- *A good self-assessment will allow you to measure your progress and compare yourself with yourself*

- *You must embrace the opinions and expertise of others in your field or who know you in order to move up*

Be Proactive | **11**

"The successful person has the habit of doing the things failures don't like to do."

–Thomas Edison
Inventor and Businessman

At the age of 22, I began using goal setting, affirmations, and visualizations. I found that my success in life was directly connected to my application of the skill I obtained. Today the people who are able to convince themselves to change by learning new technology, new skills and procedures, and even new occupations and specialties will be the most successful in the fast-changing years ahead. In order to achieve your goals and make your dreams come true you need to be proactive. Great organizations and employees have a sense of mission. An extraordinary employee actively helps lead and connects people to each other – colleague to colleague or co-worker to client. Indispensable employees follow their own lead and forge their own way forward. This proactivity allows their organization to move more quickly than it ever could if it had to wait for a paralyzed workforce to figure out the next set of rigid instructions.

Being proactive and making decisions allows you to take responsibility for yourself and your career. The

Indispensable employees follow their own lead and forge their own way forward.

only way to earn what you are truly worth is to stand out, to be seen as extraordinary, and to produce interactions that people care about. You have total control of your future if you believe in yourself and improve your performance and focus on personal excellence. Leading is a skill, not a gift. Though it may not seem like it sometimes, people aren't born with the ability to lead, they learn how to do it. Being proactive on the job will teach you to lead, and set you apart from the competition.

The only way to earn what you are truly worth is to stand out.

5 Attributes of Proactive People

1. Predict

In order to be proactive, you must learn to predict not only opportunities, but also problems and events. Begin to look for patterns; identify the normal routines and daily practices that exist. At the same time, don't allow yourself to become content. Use your skills to anticipate future outcomes. Use your creativity and logic.

2. Prevent

Proactive people prepare for potential obstacles and use their skills to find ways to overcome them before concrete roadblocks occur. Proactive people do not become overwhelmed by emotions. When challenges arise, take control and confront them head on.

3. Plan

Proactive people prepare for the future. It is essential that you avoid one-step, thinking and instead, look ahead and anticipate long-term consequences. Pull the future into the present; what can you do today to influence yourself for tomorrow? In order to make the best decision, you have to know where you came from, where you are, and where you want the destination to be.

4. Participate

Proactive people are not silent observers; they are engaging contributors.

Acknowledge that you are only a fraction of the whole and that you influence the actions of others. Engage with them. Use your influence and make a significant contribution.

5. Perform

Being proactive means taking appropriate, purposeful action. You must be willing to do the work! Procrastination is not an option; it's a failure sentence. Take control of your performance and hold yourself accountable. Learn how to accept your decisions. Know everything about your products and services better than anyone in the organization. Volunteer to fill in for other positions when employees take vacations or are sick. You will become one of the most valuable members of your organization and Move Up.

The most difficult skill that an indispensable employee must learn is delivering unique creativity and innovation. Not only do you have to have forethought and insight, you also need to find your passion and risk rejection when attempting to deliver unparalleled solutions.

The ability to learn, adjust, change course, and risk it all is the backbone of Moving Up and the indispensable employee. You need to find new solutions to problems that cause others to quit. You need to use your creativity to re-imagine opportunities and find new ways to inject yourself into them. Your instinct might be to avoid risk and solving complex problems because, "I'll get fired for breaking the rules." The extraordinary employee says, "If I take the risk, getting fired is okay, because I'll highlight my value to another organization." If a set of rules is all that stands between you and becoming indispensable and exceptional, then you don't need those rules.

If you are not proactive and searching for opportunities, you are dead in the water. You can't move up. You will stick in your current station and go no higher. You won't reach the next goal on your list. You will be forever trapped in a loop of inaction and questioning rather than making the proactive decisions necessary to move your future forward. On any job, it can be easy to waste an entire day doing nothing but busy work or mindless administrative tasks. Work that is trivial and tedious doesn't require you to lead. It doesn't require creative thinking. The challenge you face is to replace those menial tasks with proactive, rule-breaking activities that will feed your passion and lead to accomplishments you can brag about.

"That's not my job" is a phrase that can kill an entire organization. When faced with a difficult task or a complex project, try to take control of the situation. What can it hurt? Use your knowledge and skills to make informed decisions, own your assignments, and deliver quality service. Being proactive means taking the initiative to get the job done by highlighting your skills and talents.

If you are not proactive and searching for opportunities, you are dead in the water.

The extraordinary employee never says "no". An indispensable team member always finds a way, no matter what the project, no matter what the barriers, to say "yes". They find a way to make things happen. They take up the challenge and they get it done. All with a simple "yes." Say, "yes" instead of "no" as in "yes, I can solve your problem" or "yes, I can handle that project." Those employees are priceless, and they are few and far between. If you can make yourself that type of indispensable employee you will stand out in a crowd and quickly rise to the top in your organization.

The extraordinary employee never says "no".

A proactive employee on the lookout for opportunities would have seized the chance to move up. Look for opportunities to stand out all day, every day. Every interaction you have throughout the day, be it with a co-worker or client, represents an opportunity to impress others with your competence and skill level. Every product you make represents an opportunity to create something that has never been seen. Every problem situation is an opportunity to produce a positive outcome. Your customers are the reason your organization is in business at all. Employees should be able to proactively help any customer that needs their assistance.

Being proactive means taking control of your future and creating opportunities. When Moving Up you need to be prepared to do more, to overachieve, to exceed expectations, and to overcome obstacles that get in the way. You also need to be ready to crash and burn at times. Nothing ever goes perfect every time. You will fail, but you will learn from those trying moments and put those lessons into practice the next time. Trying and failing is better than just failing. Trying makes you an artist and an innovator and it gives you the right to try and try and try and try again.

Be prepared to do more, to overachieve, to exceed expectations.

To be an indispensable employee, you must understand that your job is to make things happen. This attitude will change what you do all day. When you are proactive, you make a decision that you are going to improve your own circumstances.

Look for ways to change or improve your situation by:

- *Seeking advice from others*

- *Developing your skills*

- *Setting goals*

- *Taking advantage of opportunities*

- *Learn about your products and services*

- *Exercising initiative*

These types of actions will show your clients, colleagues, and supervisors that you are a proactive employee who is ready for anything. They will be confident in your abilities and willing to listen to your opinions. They will also move your resume to the top of the stack when promotions or salary increases occur.

Consider these two employees:

Edgar works at a grocery store. He hates it. He works the cash register, and everything about him screams that he is dissatisfied with his job. Edgar refuses to make eye contact with customers and co-workers. He takes a lot of breaks and complains all the time, often right in front of customers. Edgar has decided that the job he has is beneath him and that he's not being paid enough to bring his entire self to work each day. Edgar wants to teach everyone at the store, his customer, co-workers, and owners a lesson. Melanie works at the same grocery store as Edgar. Where Edgar is despondent and checked out, Melanie is engaged and enthusiastic. She has decided that her job as a cashier is an excellent platform that she can use to make a tiny difference in the lives of the customers she serves.

The grocery store may be partially blamed for Edgar's attitude and demeanor. The organization doesn't do anything to reward employees who are generous and connected. Managers don't go out of their way to acknowledge extraordinary service or behavior. Melanie performs above and beyond. As a result, she will be leaving soon and good for her.

...your job is to make things happen.

...put yourself on display for your customers...

While Edgar is busy teaching everyone a lesson, he's teaching himself that this is the best way to do this job. He probably thinks that he will become the indispensable and extraordinary employee that he was meant to be at his next job, or his next job, or the job after that. But if he waits for a job to be good enough to deserve his best and to get him engaged, he'll probably never have that job or that chance.

When you are proactive and confident in your own skills, you put yourself on display for your customers and supervisors all the time and in every job or capacity that you find yourself in. You show others that you believe in yourself and your talents and that you can handle anything, including success. If you do great work, you will be rewarded with the knowledge you're doing something great. As a result, your day will snap into alignment with your dreams. You will be prepared to conquer bigger and better things at higher and higher levels, and you no **...believe in yourself...** longer have to pretend you're mediocre. You will be free to be extraordinary.

Personal And Professional Development

12

"Twenty years from now you will be more disappointed by the things you didn't do than by the ones you did."

–Mark Twain
Author and Humorist

I believe the greatest opportunity exists at the top. How you define the 'top' is up to you. In my many years of consulting experience, I noticed most people compete for lower level jobs. Again, I believe the reason for this is the lack of confidence. I believe your greatest opportunity for achieving your professional or personal goals is to be bold and self-confident and compete for a position above your level. Moving Up involves aiming for the top. If you believe your current state yields no room for growth, then set a goal to move to an organization that allows you to attain your objectives.

Some jobs will always pay poorly and have high turnover rates. These are jobs where showing up and pushing a button is all that really matters. The

...be bold and self-confident...

good jobs out there, the competitive jobs that you want to have are going to be filled by indispensable employees who make a difference. They will work harder than anyone else, they will set themselves apart, and they will be connected and engaged.

But how do you get there from here? How do you find those jobs and make sure you're ready? When you empower yourself to work toward your goals, be proactive, and overcome your self-imposed limitations, you can begin to further develop yourself both personally and professionally. If you are serious about investing in your future, then personal development is essential. You have to make a firm decision to spend as much time and money developing your qualifications as you do on your physical appearance. After a person graduates from school, typically no more than $1,000 of a person's own income is spent on personal development such as adult education, seminars, cd's and books. That's less than most people spend on personal appearance in one year. I recommend each year, you set aside an amount of money that you can spare to improve yourself. Attend a conference, workshop in your perspective field or a field of interest. Ultimately, if you want success you have to put in the work, which will cost you of your time and possibly financially, but the result will lead you to a better position in your career, which will lead to possible income increase.

Your self-assessment will guide you as you look for areas to strengthen and improve upon. This will help you reach your potential and stand out as an employee, a colleague, or a service provider.

Indispensable employees are not born with magical talents. They just decide that a new kind of work and attitude is important, and they use the tools at their disposal to train themselves and improve.

Never stop Learning

Since 1979, I have spent much time and money learning about customer service, the customer experience and everything related to customer service. The result has led me to position myself as the leading service strategist and expert in the world. I researched and tracked service leaders and read several business magazines each month. Every year since around 1976 I have attended the National Speakers Association Annual Conference to learn how to improve my speaking and grow my business. While the registration fee, airfare and hotel accommodations range between $1500.00-$2000.00 a year. I consider the conference to be an investment in the growth of my business. Each year, I learn something new that adds to the revenue of my business.

I have come to the conclusion that learning is the fundamental activity in a successful and purposeful life. If we fail to learn, we fail to grow, and this means that we die. Life gives us endless opportunities to learn, and the more difficult the situation, the more we are likely to learn. We can learn from other people, especially difficult ones – they are like angels sent from heaven to teach us about ourselves. We can learn from the things happening around us.

And most of all, we can learn by watching ourselves, seeing how we react and reflecting deeply on what moves us.

Your personal and professional development is your investment in your own success. Identify opportunities within your organization or through outside sources that will allow you to improve your education, enhance your skill set, or energize your passion. In order to get to the top, you have to strive to do more. I would suggest you be the first to sign-up for more work to learn more than anyone else in your department. In order to be competitive you should enthusiastically accept all the training that is available from your employer or network

In 1969, I was 21 years old; I paid $500.00 of my own money to gain access to The Dynamic of Personal Leadership program by Paul Meyers of Success Motivation Institute. Meyer believed that all people, regardless of their level of education, social class or gender, could develop the skills needed to achieve a life of success. He founded Success Motivation Institute in 1960 and dedicated his efforts to "motivating people to their full potential." He was the leading seller of personal development programs. His company developed into an international group of companies marketing his materials in more than 60 countries and in 23 languages. His books include I Inherited a Fortune, Family & Faith and the best seller, Chicken Soup for the Golden Soul.

It was an investment in my own personal development. It improved my concept of myself, helped me set my goals, and created an intense desire to succeed. You have to have a thirst for more information in whatever career field you go into.

The safest investment you or I can ever make is in us. This is how we progress. Remember, your passion isn't job or project specific. It's people specific with you right in the middle. You need to get hooked on passion and drive your success from the act of being passionate. I've had a drive to be successful, and I won't be slowing down anytime soon. People with passion in their lives look for ways to affect the outcome of their situation and make things happen. The combination of passion and work is what makes someone indispensable and unforgettable. Your personal and professional development can increase and advance your passion.

When I attended college, I spent thousands of dollars on tuition and room and board. It was not until I was out of college and got involved with Success Motivation Institute that I started to invest money in my personal development. I suggest you try to spend at least $1000.00 a year on personal development. I have spent several thousand dollars a year on personal development during my lifetime and have no intention of stopping. Consider that self-improvement book or class; perhaps enroll in a training course that will help you become more effective. Consider all of these examples as a down payment on your future. I hate to waste time. Time wasted, is time taken away from your goals. Be mindful of time snatchers. These time thieves constantly surround us. Whether it's our cell phones, email accounts, social media outlets or television. You need to be disciplined in this quest to move up in your career. You have to be willing to dedicate at least

Get hooked on passion and drive your success from the act of being passionate.

an hour a day to personal development. The return on investment could be your dreams coming true. Submerge yourself in development opportunities by turning them into concrete and measurable accomplishments. If you work diligently to get a small raise and just blow the money on something trivial, then all of your hard work will have meant nothing. Think about sinking the cash back into your own development.

Try to find unique development opportunities that will benefit you on the job and in your life in general:

- *Take an online class*

- *Buy and read a new book on personal development every month*

- *Enroll in a training course*

- *Attend a seminar or lecture with peers from your field to learn some new ideas or share your own*

- *Look for any available mentoring or training programs that enhance the skills you want*

- *Take advantage of tuition reimbursement opportunities to further your education*

You can't wait for these chances to come to you. Seek them out and take advantage of anything and everything that sparks your interest. Invest in yourself first and then put what you learn and experience to good use in accomplishing your goals.

I suggest you begin with a book-a-month objective. Commit to reading books, articles, and blogs on self-improvement at least every two weeks. Additionally, if you have any social media accounts, begin to follow people, organizations that you want to be apart of. The late Zig Ziglar, one of America's most successful motivational speakers spent three hours a day reading. If you are truly eager to succeed, you will read a broad range of books and expose yourself to the most respected people in your field or desired field, whether your field is antiques, virtual reality, cosmetology, fast food or pharmaceutical sales, it doesn't matter, each career field has room for opportunity and a mentor in that field who is positioned in a place where you want to get to.

Dress for Success

Studies show that people tend to feel great when they look great. When a person has a polished appearance, other people will take notice. Please note you cannot expect compliments to sustain your ego or equip yourself, emotionally to do good work. It is essential to compliment yourself. If you don't control what you think about yourself, someone else will. In my 20's I hired a color consultant to review my wardrobe. She was not impressed. She asked, "Do you want to look like a $20,000 speaker or just an average speaker?" I quickly changed the garments that were in my wardrobe. My clothing is a reflection of me. They tell my story before I open my mouth. All of my shirts are embroidered with customer service on the left cuff of each shirt.

If you don't control what you think about yourself, someone else will.

Exercise

If you consider yourself to be truly healthy or desire to be that way, I can tell you there is a significant difference between that level and just feeling okay. Healthy people are more energetic, alert and are peaceful in spirit. Achieving wellness has many factors; they include mental activity as well as physical, sufficient rest, proper eating habits and effective stress relieving strategies. Evaluate what kinds of changes you can make now that will enhance your physical appearance and guide you toward wellness.

Substance Abuse

Substance abuse can lead to respiratory and circulatory system breakdowns, or more severe results such as death. Substance abuse not only hurts you physically, but the damages spread to your family, friends and love ones emotionally. Two major categories of substance abuse are alcohol and drugs.

Alcohol

Large amounts of consumed alcohol over a period of time can create health conditions; such as weight gain, high blood pressure, depressed immune system and cancer. 2-4% of all cancers are closely related to alcohol. Upper digestive tract cancers are common, infecting the mouth, larynx, esophagus and pharynx. Liver disease is another high risk factor for people who drink excessively. Heavy drinking can cause fatty liver, hepatitis, cirrhosis and cancer of the liver.

Drugs

Similar to prescription drugs, illegal recreational drugs come with possible harmful side effects that can have serious long-term effects on your health. High doses of these drugs or impure substitutes can cause immediate life-threatening health problems. These problems include, heart attack, respiratory failure and coma. Mixing drugs with each other or with alcohol is extremely dangerous.

Physical

I cannot stress enough the importance of maintaining a healthy size. We live in a world where we are judged by our appearance. People who are excessively overweight may be viewed as a liability to the company. For example, if a company is a vocal advocate for healthy eating and living, yet, has employees that are obese, it makes the company look dishonest. They have to hold their employees accountable, just as much as, their customers. I believe this will play a role in whether a person is promoted or not.

Study the Part

Especially applicable to the career field are your learning abilities, thought processing patterns, problem-solving skills, beliefs, and attitudes, which are all, included in this part of the self. Thought development continues throughout one's life and is integral to career development. I believe that if you were motivated to achieve educational success, you will behave similarly on the job or in your own business. Hopefully, you have developed a high level of self-motivation. Curiosity about a number of subjects can make you a well-rounded person who is both interested and engaging. Being curious or confused and then asking meaningful questions sets the stage for learning. Asking questions on the job is expected.

Non-Verbal communication says more about us than the words we use to speak. Gestures are specific body movements that carry meaning. It is necessary to be aware of what we do with our bodies and how that can be perceived.

1. Posture:
Slouching or crossing your arms across your chest indicates boredom or anger.

2. Facial expressions:
A smile lets others know you are happy to see them.

3. Gestures:
Expansive gestures show interest.

4. Tone of voice:
Volume, pitch, pace of speaking, and vocal inflections all influence the words you are saying.

5. Eye contact:

Eye contact usually means increased comfort and trust.

6. Mannerisms:

Tapping your fingers indicates impatience.

When your physical appearance is neat and clean, people will judge your appearance as a sign of concern, responsibility and professionalism. My most difficult physical health goal is reducing my weight to 173 pounds. I am 6 feet tall. I use daily goals, visualizations and affirmations, but I love food too much. I am getting closer to my goal and that motivates me each day. How you look has a huge impact on Moving Up. If you are overweight this can lead to significant health problems and reduce your quality of life.

Good posture, great smile, eye contact, and attentiveness are all positive examples of body language that builds confidence between you and others. If you are a bit shy and have issues with giving direct eye contact or smiling, I suggest practicing in front of a mirror.

REFLECTIONS
Points to Remember

- *Indispensable employees use the tools at their disposal to train themselves and improve*

- *Use your self-assessment as a guide as you look for areas to strengthen and improve*

- *Identify opportunities within your organization or through outside sources*

- *You may need to spend some time and money on your development*

- *Seek out opportunities and take advantage of anything and everything that sparks your interest.*

The People You Know

13

"A friendship founded on business is better than a business founded on friendship."

–John D. Rockefeller
American industrialist and philanthropist

Associate only with positive, focused people who you can learn from. There's no value in settling for being a big fish in a small pool. In your journey to differentiate yourself from the competition, you may find yourself looking to others for advice, assistance, or to open doors for you. You may also find yourself judged based on the company you keep.

Associating with people you respect who value achievement and success will help you stay on the course toward your goals. There is no value to you settling for being a big fish in a small pool. Sharing in someone else's vision, or allowing them to share in yours will open up even more opportunities for you to highlight your skills and shine.

You can't always pick every person in your circles. You may be stuck with your family members, your managers, your clients, and your co-workers. You can't pick and choose their best qualities and

Associate only with positive, focused people who you can learn from.

personality traits, but you can choose whom among them to model your behavior after.

...find people who want more out of life...

Avoid modeling yourself on people who are less successful or have a negative attitude. You need to find people who want more out of life, and more money in their paycheck. You need to find people who want to move up. In my early 20s, I made the decision to associate with people who were older and more successful than I was. My mentors were dramatically more successful than me, yet they had a willingness to help and guide my potential for even larger success. I simply asked for the help, listened to their advice and implemented their suggestions

You don't always need to pick friends or mentors just because they will help you improve your career. The people within our circle of influence all provide different kinds of support at different times and for different reasons.

- *A friend can inspire you or incite a creative outburst*

- *Family members can ignite your passion and provide emotional support*

- *A mentor can provide knowledge and motivate you for success*

- *A manager can present you with improved career opportunities*

- *A supervisor can funnel complex and stimulating projects your way*

- *A team member can challenge you intellectually and invigorate your sense of competition*

When building a team, look for colleagues who fill specific roles and can work in conjunction with one another to succeed. Associate with friends, co-workers, and mentors who have positive attitudes and unique perspectives. I would also suggest you identify what you want to get out of a mentoring relationship. Not every mentoring relationship is the same. You need to know exactly what it is that you need support with, and how the mentoring relationship will benefit you. You might need help with business strategy, networking or the work-life balance. It is also notable that you find a mentor with whom you have chemistry. Don't just ask anyone into your network of mentors. You need to gel with these people.

Grow your network of mentors through your established network of associations. After you've exhausted resources among family and friends, start looking to acquaintances, colleagues, former or current employers, and others in your extended circles of influence. Approach these prospects humbly and delicately. Schedule a brief telephone conversation; limit the call to a handful of very specific questions. Hopefully, if the conversation goes well, you raise the idea of a repeat phone call. After a while, you may be able to raise the prospect of a more formal mentoring arrangement.

Positivity

...surround yourself with positive people.

If you want to be successful you need to surround yourself with positive people. Negative people will always pull you down. I think of a good friend who is quite successful. But I refuse to watch a ball game with him. He is so negative and gets down on what he calls "his team" real quick. Win or lose, I like to support my team. Maybe you are negative, and you genuinely don't realize it. I've never told my friend that I prefer not to watch the game with him; I don't want to hurt our friendship. But, I recognize that his mood affects the energy and fun of watching the game. Negative people should not suck all of your energy up.

People within your circle of influence with negative attitude damage your aspirations and can hamper your attempts to better yourself. These types of people just hold you back and slowly poison you. They tell you that it's okay to accept mediocrity, and that brainwashes the passion right out of your life.

Associate with people you respect and who are more successful

To achieve your goals you need to gravitate toward successful people with a positive attitude. When the mentors, co-workers, and friends you associate with have a positive attitude, it rubs off on you. It funnels down into your everyday life on the job and at home. You begin to look at the bright side of every situation and try to find ways to solve problems and improve outcomes. It makes you want to work harder, to become as successful as they are, and make yourself indispensable and extraordinary.

Circle of Influence Questionnaire

Use these questions to help identify those people within your circle of influence and how they help or hinder your progress and development.

1. How does this person support me emotionally?

2. How does this person support me professionally?

3. How does this person inspire me?

4. How does this person support my passion?

5. What valuable insight, knowledge, or wisdom does this person provide?

6. How does my relationship with this person positively or negatively impact me, do others perceive me based on my relationship with this person?

7. What would I be missing if this person were not in my life?

Use your answers to these questions to evaluate your relationships with your friends, family members, co-workers, and supervisors. There is no score sheet that will tell you to eliminate someone from your life, but look at the frequency of the answers you provide and utilize this information to better determine who can help you further develop and advance.

If someone seems to have an overall positive impact, seek those friends and mentors out more often for support and advice. If someone seems to have an overall negative or neutral impact, then you don't necessarily need to rely on him or her for counsel.

REFLECTIONS
Points to Remember

- *You may need to look to others for advice, assistance, or to open doors for you*

- *Associate with people you respect and who are more successful*

- *Avoid modeling yourself on people who are less successful or have a negative attitude*

- *Gravitate toward successful mentors, co-workers, and friends with positive outlooks*

Personal Mission And Vision Statement | 14

"Your life is not just about you. It's also about contributing to others. It's about living true to your mission and reason for being here on this earth at this time. It's about adding your piece of the puzzle to the world. Most people are so stuck in their egos that everything revolves around me, me, and more me. But if you want to be rich in the truest sense of the word, it can't only be about you. It has to include adding value to other people's lives"

–T. Harv Eker

Quotes from Secrets of the Millionaire Mind

Wherever you are right now, you have the opportunity to make a decisive change in your life. By now, you can see there is potential in your future; you have a thirst for wanting and achieving more.

Strategic Visioning is a developing a proactive plan for the future. It starts with (as the name implies) a vision. How will success look? What will you see? It also includes the steps for making the vision into something real.

Leaders have visions of what they want to see in the future. Each time I have an opportunity to start something, it is important that there is a clear vision; writing goal statements that match back to the vision does this. It does not matter if you are starting with a new job, moving to a new community, or preparing for the law bar exam, each milestone you begin, and you should always have a plan. Having a plan means we are laying out a blue print to achieve success. In order to do this, we must set goals for ourselves to achieve.

Brainstorming Your Vision

Step 1.   List five things you have a passion for?

Step 2.   List five things you are committed to accomplishing in your lifetime?

Step 3.   List five things you are doing right now to leverage your full potential.

Step 4.   List five priority values.

Step 5.   List ten of your strengths.

Step 6.   List five things you would like to do to make a difference in the world.

Step 7.   Look at all your answers you gave on the three pages and summarize your five life guiding principles (values).
Examples include loyalty responsibility, hard work, faith, family etc.

ASSIGNMENT: FOUNDATION HOMEWORK- MISSION STATEMENT

Write Your Vision Statement.

Paragraph 1 -	on your life guiding principles to define who you are
Paragraph 2 -	introduce five priority values (Step 4).
Paragraphs 3–7 -	describes each of these strengths in individual paragraphs (Step 5).
Paragraph 8 -	should focus on your vision based on how you answered, "What are five things you would like to do to make a difference in the world" (Step 6).

Power of the Written Goal

> **What separates extraordinary employees from mediocre ones is hard work and creative drive.**

Indispensable and extraordinary employees set goals and work tirelessly to achieve them. They don't sit on the sidelines and hope that success comes to them. Moving Up is not something done for you, but it's something you can do for yourself. There's no shortcut, but there is a clear path to becoming indispensable.

What separates extraordinary employees from mediocre ones is hard work and creative drive. Some people decide that Moving Up is significant enough to justify the extra effort. If you're one of these people, you're ready. That means first and foremost establishing your expectations.

You must have mission and vision statements in life. This is simply a set of guiding principles, which clearly state where you are going and where you want to be at the end of your life. A mission statement embodies your values. It is your personal lighthouse keeping you steadily on the course of your dreams. Whatever the mission statement of your life, refine it and review it regularly. Then when something crazy happens, or someone tries to knock you off course, you quickly and precisely return to your chosen path with the full knowledge that you are moving in the direction that you have determined.

These statements are enthusiastic declarations that simply and succinctly convey your overall personal objectives and direction. A clear and concise mission statement and vision statement can powerfully communicate your intentions and motivate you to realize an inspiring personal vision of the future.

A Mission Statement defines your purpose and primary objectives. It outlines the key measures of your success and leads to practical application. A Vision Statement also defines your purpose, but in terms of your values and guiding beliefs. There are no concrete measures, but it creates a baseline that all future goals and aspirations fit inside. It shapes your understanding of what you work for, what inspires you, and what success means to you.

Use these two documents to maintain the level of quality in your work and motivate you when difficulties arise (and they will).

Mission Statement Creation

1. Identify your inspired idea or life's goal

2. Identify the key measures of your success
   - choose the most important measures and keep it uncomplicated

3. Combine your inspired idea and success measures into a tangible goal statement - refine it until you have a precise statement of your personal mission, which expresses your ideas and desired results

Consider the following example:

"To become the top high-end computer salesperson by selling the highest quality, most technologically advanced, user friendly equipment. Maintain 98% customer satisfaction and increase salary by 35% in the next four years."

The Big Picture | 15

"Details create the big picture."

–Sanford I. Weill
(former chairman and chief executive of Citigroup)

The one trait that best marks a winner is perseverance – a winner never quits. Never give in to the idea that your dreams are too big. You may experience delays along the way, but not cancellations.

We all have passions, but not everyone can experience those passions through their work. Do not muddle along any longer, wondering why you haven't succeeded. I believe people benefit from unlearning behaviors and attitudes that have been ineffective for them, thereby creating intellectual space for new learning. One clear path to success is to merge our work and passion. When viewing the big picture, it's important to ask: how do I practice my passion in the work that I do?

...a winner never quits.

When setting your goals in the short term, whether you want to get a raise or a promotion, don't take your eye off of the big picture. What is it that you ultimately want to do with your life? What will make you happy? Where do you want to go? What do you dream of doing? Every smaller goal you accomplish should feed into the larger, long-term goals that you have for yourself.

How is that raise going to help you? What are you going to do with the money? What opportunities will open up for you when you get that promotion? How will those opportunities continue to propel you forward?

Set NEW goals. Dream bigger.

When you get a raise, take some of that extra income and invest in your own future. Put your job to work for you. Make every customer encounter, performance review, or project a public display of your expertise and proficiency. Use your experiences as learning opportunities that will help you get to the next level in your quest.

Once you reach a desired goal, keep going. Set NEW goals. Dream bigger. Think twenty or thirty years down the road. Don't get complacent with your life or your position. There's nothing wrong with wanting more. Don't ever settle. You can always work harder, make more money, improve your situation, and live the dream. Remember that believing is the first step toward making those dreams a reality.

Don't ever settle.

By keeping the big picture in mind, you can construct a series of manageable goals that will help you get there. If your first goal is to get a raise, how do you get there? Can you increase your efficiency and focus on eliminating mistakes? Can you improve your customer feedback scores? Can you be more proactive in seeking out additional projects? What small steps can you make to set yourself apart to achieve your short-term goals? It's interesting to distinguish jobs from work. We all have jobs, but work is something we do with our heart and soul. To be indispensable means taking risks, being extraordinary and creative. To be successful, we have to consider the big picture. We need to weave the success in our past, the aspirations of our future and the passions we feel today. When we feel passionate, we care enough about working hard to Move Up. That's why it's so important to merge our work with our passion or to find passion in our work. Passion also drives us to persist as we work toward Moving Up.

You don't move up and get promoted just because you show up and really "want" a new position. You need to make yourself more valuable, more indispensable. Think about what you can do or learn that can fill an unmet need in your organization. What 5 or 10 things do you need to improve about yourself to become more valuable? Everyone can be extraordinary and indispensable. Think of a time when you stood out – when you were extraordinary, creative, and your success was recognized. Let that be a model for your success – remember how you felt. Everyone wants to feel the accolades that accompany success.

To be indispensable means taking risks, being extraordinary and creative.

You need to make yourself more valuable, more indispensable.

Everyone can be extraordinary and indispensable.

Conclusion | **16**

"Greatness is not a function of circumstance. Greatness, it turns out, is largely a matter of conscious choice and discipline."

–Jim Collins
American business consultant, author and lecturer

You have the power to choose your experience. You also need to accept that power as a responsibility. Our behavior is a natural outcome of our mental thoughts, and so we are responsible for our actions too, and also for the way we allow others to treat us. If we allow others to ride roughshod over us, then we have ourselves to blame.

Now that you understand that you will be rewarded for standing out, for making connections, and for being remarkable, what are you going to do?

You have a genius, an artist, and an innovator inside of you. You have something to share with the world. We all do. Are you going to keep it under wraps, hold back, and settle for less than you deserve just because you're afraid?

You have a genius, an artist, and an innovator inside of you.

You need to stand for something and make a difference in your life and the lives of the people around you. Over the course of Moving Up, we discussed many topics that can help you become the type of indispensable and extraordinary employee who expects and embraces success:

- *An honest belief in yourself and your abilities is the first step to making your dreams a reality*

- *Set goals that are manageable and measurable to help you put your priorities in order and create a roadmap to success*

- *Overcome your fears and self-imposed limitations in order to realize your potential and sidestep any barriers in your way*

- *Examine your talents and deficiencies with an objective self-assessment*

- *Be proactive to create opportunities set yourself apart from the competition*

- *Dedicate yourself to a strict regime of personal and professional development*

- *Maintain quality association and rely on exceptional and qualified job mentors to help you on your way*

- *Accept success. Yes, you are worthy of Moving Up*

The only thing keeping you from being exceptional and indispensable is your own determination. Others may tell you that you can't possibly do it. You may even hear yourself say that you don't deserve it. Those close to you may even laugh at times, but your determination to overcome that resistance will show everyone – even yourself. By making the choice to overcome these challenges and having the insight to set the right goals and draw the best map, you can become a truly indispensable employee that any organization would be lucky to employ.

You can sit and be invisible, or you can stand out.

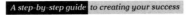

If you have thoughts, comments, or ideas about this book, I'd love to hear from you. Feel free to write or call me.

John Tschohl
Service Quality Institute
9201 East Bloomington Freeway
Minneapolis, Minnesota 55420-3497 USA
952-884-3311 fax 952-884-8901
Email: **quality@servicequality.com**
Web-site: **www.customer-service.com**

Service Quality Institute provides a variety of customer service programs that can help your organization create a service culture and develop high performing employees. Our products change behaviors and attitudes and teach the art and skills of customer service while building employee morale and facilitating teamwork. All of our programs are based on achieving awesome service through recognition. In addition to this book, Service Quality Institute offers a structured training program, Moving Up, that you can use to train your total workforce.

If you are interested in learning more about Service Quality Institute's training programs or about John Tschohl's seminars and speeches, please contact Service Quality Institute at the above address.

ALSO BY JOHN TSCHOHL

EMPOWERMENT: A WAY OF LIFE
(Best Sellers Publishing, 2010) **ISBN: 978-0-9826369-0-09, $19.**95)

ACHIEVING EXCELLENCE THROUGH CUSTOMER SERVICE
(Best Sellers Publishing, 2008, **ISBN: 0-9636268-4-4, $19.**95)

LOYAL FOR LIFE
(Best Sellers Publishing, 2005, **ISBN: 0-9636268-8-4, $14.**95)

E-SERVICE
(Best Sellers Publishing, 2001, **ISBN: 0-9636268-6-8, $24.**95)

CA$HING IN
(Best Sellers Publishing, 1995, **ISBN: 0-9636268-2-5, $14.**95)

THE CUSTOMER IS BOSS
(Best Sellers Publishing, 1993, **ISBN: 0-9636268-0-9, $19.**95)

These books and additional copies of **Moving Up** are available in local bookstores. For volume orders, contact Best Sellers Publishing at 952-888-7672 or by e-mail. If you want an empowered workforce, you should introduce a new training program on customer service at least every four to six months. There is no magic bullet or book that will change an individual's life. Repetition and reinforcement are critical to getting your entire staff to be customer driven.

For more information to offer comments or ask questions, please email us at **BSP@BestSellersPublishing.com**